# NO-PREP SLOW COOKER

# NO-PREP SLOW COOKER

*easy, few-ingredient meals*
without the Browning, Sautéing
or Pre-Baking

## CHRISSY TAYLOR

*founder of* The Taylor House

PAGE STREET
PUBLISHING CO.

PAGE STREET
PUBLISHING CO.

First published in 2017 by

Page Street Publishing Co.

27 Congress Street, Suite 105

Salem, MA 01970

www.pagestreetpublishing.com

Distributed by Macmillan, sales in Canada by The Canadian Manda Group.

21  20  19  18  17      1  2  3  4  5

ISBN-13: 978-1-62414-427-1

ISBN-10: 1-62414-427-6

Library of Congress Control Number: 2017931838

Cover and book design by Page Street Publishing Co.

Photography by Ted Axelrod

Printed and bound in China

As a member of 1% for the Planet, Page Street Publishing protects our planet by donating to nonprofits like The Trustees, which focuses on local land conservation. Learn more at onepercentfortheplanet.org.

This book is dedicated to my three guys: Eric, Joey and Blake.

# CONTENTS

# PREFACE

Hello, friends. I have been blessed to be married for twenty years to my amazing husband, Eric. Together we have two wonderful boys, Joey and Blake. Being a wife and mom, creating a place to call home and having meals on the table every evening for my sweet family is all I ever wanted in this life.

I've always had a passion for being in the kitchen. As I was growing up, my mom let me help her make everything from potato soup and homemade bread to chili and Christmas cookies. The recipes I grew up making inspired me to put a twist on them and share the new versions with my family.

Slow cooker recipes have always been a favorite of mine. I love to put ingredients in a pot and let them cook on their own for several hours. It gives your house a delicious aroma, and you end up with a simple meal that took such a small amount of work. It's almost become a fun game, figuring out how to make a traditional recipe in the slow cooker and have it come out tasty and with the perfect texture. The fewer the ingredients, the better!

These slow cooker recipes are always a big hit on my blog, The Taylor House. I love making them not just for my family, but for my readers, too. I've been able to turn a love and hobby of cooking into a business, helping parents with a busy part of their lives, raising kids and getting a delicious dinner on the table with little work. In the end, you'll be spending more time with your kids and less time working in the kitchen.

I'm incredibly grateful you've picked up this book to try new recipes. I hope you find them easy to make while bringing comfort and happiness to your dinner table when you share them with your family.

# A WELL-STOCKED PANTRY

A well-stocked pantry will help keep your ingredients list short so you can run in and out of the store in no time at all!

Here are some items that I keep on hand at all times and will make for a most efficient pantry, refrigerator and spice rack. In each recipe, I've bolded other ingredients that you'll need to purchase.

## Pantry

- Bread crumbs
- Broth (chicken, beef, vegetable)
- Brown sugar
- Cooking wine or regular wine (red, white, sherry, Marsala)
- Cornstarch
- Diced tomatoes
- Flour
- Honey
- Olive oil
- Pasta (elbow, shells)
- Peanut butter
- Rice
- Sugar
- Vinegars (apple cider, white)
- Worcestershire sauce

## Refrigerator

- Butter
- Carrots
- Cream cheese
- Eggs
- Fresh herbs (parsley, cilantro)
- Garlic, minced
- Ketchup
- Lemons
- Mayonnaise
- Milk
- Mustard (Dijon)
- Onions
- Sour cream or plain yogurt

## Spices

- Bay leaves
- Cayenne pepper
- Chili powder
- Cinnamon
- Cumin
- Dried basil
- Dried oregano
- Dried parsley
- Garlic powder
- Italian seasoning blend
- Onion powder
- Paprika
- Pepper
- Red pepper flakes
- Salt
- Vanilla extract

# Full-Flavor
# FANTASTIC
# CHICKEN

Tired of making the same chicken recipes over and over again but don't know where to look for new inspiration? My slow cooker chicken recipes are not just simple to make, but they also pack a punch when it comes to flavor. Your family will love the new take on some of the traditional recipes. You'll appreciate their simplicity, allowing you to spend more time with your family and friends.

# CHICKEN MARSALA ⊙

One of my favorite dishes to order when I'm at a restaurant is chicken marsala. After begging my husband to take me out over and over again, I decided it was time to make my own version. This is a recipe that will impress your family and guests with the restaurant-quality flavors you can make right at home.

**MAKES 4 TO 6 SERVINGS**

4 to 6 **chicken breasts**

1 cup (240 ml) Marsala wine

1 lb (454 g) **mushrooms**

½ cup (120 ml) water

2 tsp (6 g) garlic, minced

1 tsp fresh parsley

Pasta, rice or **mashed potatoes**, for serving

Place the chicken breasts in the slow cooker. In a medium-size bowl, mix together the Marsala wine, mushrooms, water, garlic and parsley. Pour the mixture over the chicken.

Cook on low for 6 hours.

Serve over pasta, rice or mashed potatoes.

# CREAMY ITALIAN CHICKEN

This isn't your normal creamy chicken recipe—it's the one you'll turn to again and again because it's full of mind-blowing flavors. Adding hearty mushrooms and fresh lemon gives this recipe a whole new twist.

**MAKES 4 SERVINGS**

4 **chicken breasts**, thawed

½ cup (115 g) butter

4 oz (114 g) cream cheese

1 (10-oz (283-g]) can **cream of mushroom soup**

2 tbsp (30 ml) fresh lemon juice

1 cup (66 g) **fresh mushrooms**, sliced

White rice, noodles or **mashed potatoes**, for serving

Place the chicken breasts in the bottom of the slow cooker. In a medium-size bowl, melt the butter in the microwave for 30 seconds or until it is mostly melted. Add the cream cheese to the melted butter and microwave for an additional 30 seconds. After the butter and cream cheese mixture is melted and mixed, stir in the cream of mushroom soup (do not add water), lemon juice and mushrooms. Mix everything together well and pour it over the chicken breasts.

Cook on low for 6 to 8 hours.

Serve over white rice, noodles or mashed potatoes.

# ◐ SALSA LIME CHICKEN

There're often times when I need a recipe to deliver to friends or family during occasions such as illnesses and births, and this Salsa Lime Chicken is the perfect meal. It's simple to make and everyone loves it! The hint of lime combined with the flavor of zesty salsa makes this a recipe you will want to keep handy!

**MAKES 4 TO 6 SERVINGS**

4 to 6 chicken breasts

1 (16-oz [454-g]) jar salsa

½ cup (120 ml) lime juice

1 (1-oz [28-g]) packet taco seasoning mix

Rice, optional, for serving

Fresh cilantro, optional, for serving

Place the chicken breasts in the slow cooker. In a medium-size bowl, combine the salsa, lime juice and taco seasoning. Pour the mixture into the slow cooker and cover.

Cook on low for 6 hours or on high for 4 hours.

Serve the whole chicken breast over rice or shred and use in burritos. Top with fresh cilantro.

# FIESTA CHICKEN

Fiesta Chicken is a delicious recipe that we make when we're craving tacos but want something a little different. Shredding the chicken makes it perfect to serve on tortillas, over rice or even on a bun.

**MAKES 4 TO 6 SERVINGS**

4 to 6 chicken breasts

1 (15-oz [425-g]) can black beans

1 (14.5-oz [411-g]) can diced tomatoes

1 (15-oz [425-g]) can corn (do not drain)

1 (8-oz [227-g]) package cream cheese

1 (1-oz [28-g]) packet ranch dip

Tortillas, rice or buns, for serving

Peppers and onions, optional

Place the chicken breasts in the slow cooker. Add the black beans, diced tomatoes and corn. Combine the cream cheese and ranch dip packet in a small bowl. Add to the slow cooker.

Cook for 4 to 6 hours on low.

Shred the chicken with a fork and serve on a tortilla, over rice or on a bun. Spice this dish up by adding peppers and onions.

# CHICKEN CARNITAS

This Chicken Carnitas recipe is easy to make your own way by adjusting the spice level to your preference.
If you love heat, add more chili powder and cumin, or keep it mild by going with a little less.

**MAKES 4 TO 6 SERVINGS**

4 to 6 chicken breasts

1 (12-oz [340-ml]) can beer

1 small onion, diced

2 tbsp (20 g) garlic, minced

2 tsp (5 g) chili powder

1 tsp cumin

Tacos or tortillas, for serving

Place the chicken breasts in the slow cooker. Add the beer, onion, garlic, chili powder and cumin.

Cook on low for 6 to 8 hours or on high for 4 to 5 hours. Shred the chicken with a fork.

Serve in tacos or tortillas.

# CHICKEN POT PIE STEW

Turn your favorite comfort food into stew. One bite of this meal brings back a flood of memories from my childhood and days spent around the table with Mom and Dad. It's the perfect cozy meal to keep you warm on a cool day.

**MAKES 4 TO 6 SERVINGS**

3 chicken breasts, diced

1 (16-oz [454-g]) bag mixed veggies

1 cup (240 ml) chicken broth

1 tsp garlic, minced

4 tbsp (57 g) butter

4 tbsp (30 g) flour

1 cup (240 ml) milk

Biscuits, for serving

Place the chicken breasts in the slow cooker. Add the vegetables, chicken broth and garlic.

Cook on low for 6 hours.

In a small saucepan, melt the butter over medium heat. Whisk in the flour until well-blended to make a roux, approximately 5 minutes. Add the milk. Pour the mixture into the slow cooker. Continue cooking on low for 30 minutes.

Serve with biscuits.

# ONE-POT CHICKEN AND VEGGIES

A delicious one-pot meal is a treasure. As a busy mom, I love nothing more than a meal with only a few dishes to wash! This One-Pot Chicken and Veggies is just that—everything goes in the slow cooker, and your meal is ready in a few hours. I end up with an easy, home-style cooked meal the whole family will enjoy.

**MAKES 4 SERVINGS**

4 chicken breasts

3 cups (450 g) green beans

4 cups (600 g) red potatoes, diced

½ cup (120 ml) lemon juice

3 tbsp (45 ml) melted butter

2 tbsp (20 g) garlic, minced

1 tbsp (3 g) parsley

Biscuits, for serving

Place all the ingredients in the slow cooker.

Cook on low for 6 to 8 hours or on high for 4 to 6 hours.

Serve with fresh biscuits.

# SEASONED WHOLE CHICKEN

This Seasoned Whole Chicken is not only a great recipe for weeknights, but it's a delicious alternative to turkey as well and can be made for the holidays. I like to make a chicken at the beginning of the week and use it in sandwiches, salads and recipes throughout the week.

**MAKES 6 TO 8 SERVINGS**

1 (4 lb [1.8 kg]) **small chicken**

1 small onion, sliced

1 lemon, sliced

1 tsp garlic

1 tsp **seasoning salt**

1 tsp parsley

Put balls of tin foil in the bottom of the slow cooker. Place the chicken on top of the foil. Place the sliced onion and lemon on top of the chicken. Mix the seasonings together and cover the chicken.

Cook on low for 8 hours or on high for 4 to 6 hours.

# ZESTY BBQ CHICKEN SANDWICH

I like making this recipe for potlucks and crowds. It's just one of those meals that goes over well—and everyone asks for the recipe so they can make it themselves!

**MAKES 8 TO 10 SERVINGS**

4 to 6 **chicken breasts**

1 cup (240 ml) **BBQ sauce**

1 cup (240 ml) **Italian dressing**

2 tbsp (20 g) **brown sugar**

**Buns**, for serving

Place the chicken breasts in the slow cooker. In a small-size bowl, combine the BBQ sauce, Italian dressing and brown sugar. Pour the mixture over the chicken.

Cook on low for 6 hours or on high for 3 to 4 hours. Shred with a fork.

Serve on a bun.

# GRANDMA'S CHICKEN AND NOODLES

There's one recipe that my grandma is known for and that's chicken noodles. It has everything that a comfort recipe needs. This is my take on Grandma's Chicken Noodles, and it's best served over mashed potatoes. This is the most popular recipe on the Taylor House blog, too!

**MAKES 6 TO 8 SERVINGS**

. . . . . . . . . . . . . . . . . . . . . . . . . . . . . . . . . . . . . . . . . . . . . . . . . . . . . . . . .

4 **chicken breasts**, cooked and diced

2 (14.5-oz [411-ml]) cans chicken broth

2 (10-oz [283-g]) cans **cream of chicken soup**

4 oz (115 g) butter

1 tbsp (10 g) garlic, minced

1 (12- to 16-oz [340- to 454-g]) package **egg noodles**

Mashed potatoes, optional, for serving

Place the chicken breasts, broth, soup, butter and garlic in the slow cooker.

Cook on low for 6 to 8 hours or on high for 4 to 6 hours. Add the noodles to the slow cooker 30 minutes before the dish is done.

Serve over mashed potatoes.

# ORANGE SESAME CHICKEN

Treat your taste buds to this rich, flavorful Orange Sesame Chicken. We love Chinese takeout, but it can get expensive. This Orange Sesame Chicken is a great alternative to ordering out.

**MAKES 4 TO 6 SERVINGS**

4 chicken breasts, diced

1 cup (245 g) orange marmalade

1 cup (240 ml) BBQ sauce

2 tbsp (30 ml) soy sauce

Chives, for serving

White rice, for serving

Place the chicken breasts in the slow cooker. In a small-size bowl, mix the marmalade, BBQ sauce and soy sauce. Pour the mixture into the slow cooker and cover the chicken.

Cook on low for 6 to 8 hours or on high for 4 hours.

Top with chives and serve over white rice.

# CHICKEN STIR-FRY NOODLES

Chicken and fresh veggies make this Chinese dish a favorite that you can prepare right in your slow cooker! Serve on white or fried rice for a complete meal.

**MAKES 4 TO 6 SERVINGS**

1 lb (454 g) mushrooms

3 chicken breasts, diced

2 cups (350 g) broccoli

1 cup (110 g) carrots, shredded

2 (3-oz [85-g]) packages ramen noodles

4 tbsp (60 ml) stir-fry sauce

2 cups (473 ml) chicken broth

Rice, for serving

In a large-size bowl, combine the mushrooms, chicken breasts, broccoli, carrots and ramen noodles. Place the mixture into the slow cooker. Add the stir-fry sauce and chicken broth.

Cook on low for 6 to 8 hours or on high for 4 hours.

Serve over rice.

# Mind-Blowing
## BEEF

Finding recipes you can make again and again for your family is something all moms wish for. We strive for the trifecta: meals that we love, are easy to make and our kids will eat without complaining. These mind-blowing beef recipes are exactly what you're looking for. Many of the recipes are a new take on old favorites that will get you excited to bring them back to your menu.

# SALISBURY STEAK MEATBALLS ➡

Salisbury steak is a meal that I grew up on. I remember my mom making it often, and there was nothing better than that delicious steak and gravy over creamy homemade mashed potatoes. I've given this regular recipe a makeover with this mouthwatering twist!

**MAKES 6 TO 8 SERVINGS**

1 (26-oz (737-g]) bag frozen meatballs

2 (10-oz (283-g]) cans cream of mushroom soup

1 (1-oz [28-g]) package au jus mix

½ cup (120 ml) water

Mashed potatoes, for serving

Place the meatballs in the slow cooker. In a medium-size bowl, whisk the soup, au jus mix and water together. Pour it over the meatballs.

Cook on low for 6 to 8 hours or on high for 3 to 4 hours.

Serve over mashed potatoes.

# EASY TACO LASAGNA

Taco and lasagna, all in one delicious recipe! Add a side salad and some buttery garlic bread for an amazing meal your family will ask for again and again.

**MAKES 4 TO 6 SERVINGS**

1 lb (454 g) ground beef

1 small onion, diced

½ cup (120 ml) water

1 (1-oz [28-g]) packet taco seasoning

1 (24-oz [709-ml]) jar spaghetti sauce

1 (25-oz [709-g]) package frozen cheese-filled ravioli

2 cups (241 g) shredded mozzarella cheese

In a medium-size skillet, cook the beef for 8 to 10 minutes or until the meat is brown. Add the onion, water and taco seasoning to the beef. Stir in the spaghetti sauce. Place the ravioli in the slow cooker. Pour the beef and sauce mixture over the ravioli and top with cheese.

Cook on low for 4 hours.

*Note:*

If you're short on time, you can place the ground beef and onion in the slow cooker without browning. Simply follow all the other steps in the recipe the same way. The texture of the recipe may be slightly altered with this change, but it will still be delicious!

# BACON CHEESEBURGER MEAT LOAF

Combining two dinner favorites into one amazing meal is a recipe for success!
Meat loaf leftovers are perfect for making sandwiches the day after.

**MAKES 6 TO 8 SERVINGS**

2 lb (907 g) ground beef

1 small onion, diced

½ cup (29 g) bread crumbs

½ cup (118 ml) BBQ sauce, plus more
for serving

1 tbsp (15 ml) Worcestershire sauce

2 cups (241 g) cheddar cheese

4 slices bacon, cooked and chopped

Mix the beef, onion, bread crumbs, BBQ sauce and Worcestershire sauce in a
large-size bowl until well-combined. Shape the mixture into a rectangle, 1 inch
(2.5 cm) thick. Sprinkle the cheese down the center and top with bacon. Mold the
beef around the cheese and bacon. Place it in the slow cooker.

Cook on low for 4 hours.

Top with extra BBQ sauce.

# SHREDDED BEEF BURRITOS

Slow cooker shredded beef makes the best burritos! Cooking the meat low and slow for several hours makes it incredibly tender and flavorful. You won't need to go out to order this meal anymore!

**MAKES 6 TO 8 SERVINGS**

1 (5 lb [2.5 kg]) chuck roast

1 (14.5-oz [411-ml]) container beef broth

1 tsp garlic salt

1 (1-oz [28-g]) packet taco seasoning

Tortillas and toppings (lettuce, cheese, tomatoes, guacamole, salsas and sour cream), for serving

Place the roast in the slow cooker. Add the broth, garlic salt and taco seasoning.

Cook on low for 8 to 10 hours. Shred with a fork.

Serve with tortillas and optional toppings like lettuce, cheese, tomatoes, guacamole, salsas and sour cream.

# RED WINE POT ROAST

The perfect pot roast recipe is a must-have in your recipe collection. There's nothing like a fall-apart roast with a creamy gravy to serve over mashed potatoes or rice. Using red wine in your roast gives it a whole new layer of flavor your taste buds will love.

**MAKES 4 TO 6 SERVINGS**

3 lb (1.5 kg) beef roast

½ cup (120 ml) red wine

½ cup (120 ml) beef broth

1 (1-oz [28-g]) package mushroom gravy

1 lb (454 g) mushrooms, sliced

Mashed potatoes or rice, for serving

Place the beef roast in the slow cooker. In a small-size bowl, combine the wine, broth and gravy. Pour it over the roast. Add the sliced mushrooms to the slow cooker.

Cook on low for 8 hours or on high for 6 hours.

Serve with mashed potatoes or rice.

# HOMEMADE CHEESEBURGER MACARONI

Forget mac and cheese out of the box—this homemade version will be a hit with everyone at the dinner table. Kick it up a notch by making it a cheeseburger mac and cheese!

**MAKES 4 TO 6 SERVINGS**

1 lb (454 g) ground beef

1 onion, diced

1 green bell pepper, diced

1 tsp garlic, minced

2 cups (473 ml) beef broth

1 (15-oz [425-g]) can tomato sauce

3 cups (348 g) elbow pasta, uncooked

2 cups (241 g) shredded cheddar cheese, for serving

In a medium-size skillet, cook the beef for 8 to 10 minutes or until brown. Place the beef in the slow cooker with the onion, pepper, garlic, broth and sauce.

Cook on low for 6 to 8 hours or on high for 3 to 4 hours.

Add the pasta to the slow cooker 30 minutes before the dish is done. Top with a sprinkle of cheese.

*Note:*

If you're short on time, you can place the ground beef in the slow cooker without browning. Simply follow all the other steps in the recipe the same way. The texture of the recipe may be slightly altered with this change, but it will still be delicious!

# TACO FIESTA
# BUBBLE PIZZA

Find your family's new favorite recipe with this taco and pizza combination meal. Using easy refrigerated biscuits in this dish makes it a hit with moms and kids alike. Personalize this recipe for your family by adding their favorite toppings.

**MAKES 4 TO 6 SERVINGS**

2 (16.3-oz [462-g]) cans refrigerated biscuits (I prefer large Grands)

1 lb (454 g) ground beef

1 (1-oz [28-g]) packet taco seasoning

1 (14-oz [396-g]) jar pizza sauce

1 cup (121 g) Mexican blend cheese

1 (14.5-oz [411-g]) can diced tomatoes

Sour cream, for serving

Cut the biscuits into quarters and place them in the slow cooker. In a medium-size skillet, cook the beef for 8 to 10 minutes or until brown. Add the taco seasoning and pizza sauce to the beef and mix them together. Pour the beef mixture over the biscuits. Add the cheese and tomatoes.

Cook on low for 2 to 4 hours or on high for 1 to 2 hours.

Serve with sour cream.

*Note:*

If you're short on time, you can place the ground beef in the slow cooker without browning. Simply follow all the other steps in the recipe the same way. The texture of the recipe may be slightly altered with this change, but it will still be delicious!

# SHREDDED BEEF PHILLY CHEESE STEAK SANDWICH

Philly cheese steak sandwiches are my oldest son's favorite sandwich. Whenever we go out to eat, this is what he looks for to order. I love that I can make his favorite dish at home with this simple recipe.

**MAKES 6 TO 8 SERVINGS**

2 lb (907 g) round steak, thinly sliced

1 onion, sliced

1 bell pepper, sliced

2 cups (473 ml) beef broth

1 (1-oz [28-g]) packet Italian dressing mix

French rolls and provolone cheese, for serving

Place all of the ingredients except for the French rolls and provolone cheese in the slow cooker.

Cook on low for 6 hours.

Serve on French rolls and top with provolone cheese.

# BACON CHEESEBURGERS

Just because the weather isn't right for grilling doesn't mean you can't enjoy a mouthwatering cheeseburger. This slow cooker version is packed with flavor that will keep your family coming back for seconds.

**MAKES 4 TO 6 SERVINGS**

2 lb (907 g) ground beef

¼ lb (113 g) bacon, cooked and crumbled

1 small onion, diced

8 oz (227 g) soft cheese (I prefer Velveeta)

1 tsp garlic, minced

Burger buns and toppings (lettuce, tomato, onion), for serving

In a medium-size skillet, cook the beef for 8 to 10 minutes or until brown. Place the beef in the slow cooker. Add the bacon, onion, cheese and garlic.

Cook on low for 6 hours or on high for 4 hours. Stir every hour.

Place on buns and top with your favorite burger fixings!

*Note:*

If you're short on time, you can place the ground beef in the slow cooker without browning. Simply follow all the other steps in the recipe the same way. The texture of the recipe may be slightly altered with this change, but it will still be delicious!

# HAMBURGER HASH WITH CHEESE

I can throw this recipe together in a snap because I always have the ingredients on hand. Hamburger hash is a creamy casserole dish that's full of potatoes, beans and, of course, cheese!

**MAKES 4 TO 6 SERVINGS**

3 cups (450 g) russet potatoes

1 lb (454 g) lean ground beef

1 white onion

2 (10-oz [284-g]) cans cream of mushroom soup

1 (15-oz [425-g]) can green beans

2 cups (241 g) shredded cheddar cheese

Salt and pepper

Dice the potatoes and onion into bite-size pieces. Layer the potatoes across the bottom of the slow cooker.

In a medium-size skillet, brown the ground beef and onion over medium heat until the onion is translucent, about 5 minutes. Mix the cream of mushroom soup and green beans into the beef mixture until the meat is creamy and coated with the soup. Pour the mixture into the slow cooker and cover the potatoes evenly.

Cook on low for 6 to 8 hours. Add the cheese, salt and pepper to taste 30 minutes before the dish is done.

*Note:*

If you're short on time, you can place the ground beef and onion in the slow cooker without browning. Simply follow all the other steps in the recipe the same way. The texture of the recipe may be slightly altered with this change, but it will still be delicious!

# BBQ SLOPPY JOES

Sloppy joes are on our menu at least every other week. This is a simple recipe that takes no time to put together, and preparing sloppy joes in the slow cooker makes them a great option for serving guests. We like to make a double batch of these BBQ Sloppy Joes on days we're watching football games.

**MAKES 6 TO 8 SERVINGS**

2 lb (907 g) ground beef, cooked

1 medium onion, diced

2 cups (473 ml) BBQ sauce

1 cup (240 ml) ketchup

½ cup (110 g) brown sugar

1¼ cups (296 ml) apple cider vinegar

2 tbsp (30 ml) Dijon mustard

1 tbsp (10 g) garlic, minced

Buns, for serving

In a medium-size skillet, cook the beef for 8 to 10 minutes or until brown. Add the diced onion to the beef and cook until it's translucent, about 5 minutes. Place the beef and onion in the slow cooker. In a medium-size bowl, mix the BBQ sauce, ketchup, brown sugar, vinegar, mustard and garlic. Pour the mixture into the slow cooker and stir it into the beef.

Cook on low for 6 to 8 hours or on high for 4 to 6 hours.

Serve on buns.

*Note:*

If you're short on time, you can place the ground beef and onion in the slow cooker without browning. Simply follow all the other steps in the recipe the same way. The texture of the recipe may be slightly altered with this change, but it will still be delicious!

# Simply
# DELICIOUS
# PORK

My brother is someone who seems to be able to throw a bunch of ingredients together without much planning and have them turn into something delicious. He's always using different cuts of pork for his recipes, which has inspired me to create these delicious recipes for you to try with your family.

# SWEET-AND-SPICY PULLED PORK

This tasty pork sandwich is the perfect recipe to make for parties and gatherings. Everyone will love its delicious sweet flavor with just a hint of spice. If you're looking for a recipe to serve a crowd, this is the perfect pick!

**MAKES 6 TO 8 SERVINGS**

2 lb (907 g) pork roast

2 tbsp (28 g) brown sugar

2 cups (480 ml) BBQ sauce

1 tsp garlic, minced

1 tsp cayenne pepper

1 tsp chili powder

1 tsp cumin

Buns, for serving

Place the pork roast in the slow cooker. In a medium-size bowl, mix the brown sugar, BBQ sauce, garlic, pepper, chili powder and cumin. Pour the mixture over the pork roast.

Cook on low for 6 to 8 hours or on high for 4 to 6 hours. Shred with a fork.

Serve on fresh buns.

# BBQ RIBS

There is nothing more delicious and satisfying than a plate of BBQ Ribs. My husband loves good ribs, so we went the extra mile to find the perfect recipe for making BBQ Ribs in the slow cooker!

2 tbsp (28 g) brown sugar

1 tbsp (7 g) paprika

1 tbsp (15 g) salt

5 lb (2.5 kg) baby back ribs

3 cups (710 ml) BBQ sauce

Mix the dry ingredients together and rub them on the meaty side of the ribs. Place the ribs in the slow cooker. Cover all sides of the ribs with BBQ sauce.

Cook on low for 6 to 8 hours.

# PORK MUSHROOM STROGANOFF

Stroganoff on a whole new level of good! Try making this traditional recipe with pork meat instead of beef for a new flavor and texture. Adding the ranch dressing mix to the recipe gives the dish an amazing flavor.

1 lb (454 g) pork stew meat

2 (10-oz [284-g]) cans cream of mushroom soup

2 cups (133 g) fresh mushrooms, sliced

1 (1-oz [28-g]) packet ranch dressing mix

Place the meat in the slow cooker. In a medium-size bowl, mix the soup, mushrooms and ranch dressing mix. Pour the mixture over the pork stew meat.

Cook on low for 6 hours or on high for 4 hours.

# SMOTHERED PORK CHOPS

Transform plain pork chops into a mouthwatering dinner by adding creamy mushroom soup and cheese.
Serve with mashed potatoes to make this a meal you won't forget.

**MAKES 4 TO 6 SERVINGS**

4 to 6 pork chops

2 (10-oz [284-g]) cans cream of mushroom soup

1 (1-oz [28-g]) packet onion soup mix

½ cup (120 ml) water

2 cups (241 g) cheddar cheese

Mashed potatoes, for serving

Spray the slow cooker with a nonstick cooking spray. Lay the pork chops in the bottom of the slow cooker. In a medium-size bowl, mix together the soup, soup mix and water. Pour the mixture over the pork chops. Top with cheese.

Cook on low for 7 to 8 hours or on high for 4 to 5 hours.

Serve with mashed potatoes.

# DIJON MUSTARD PORK CHOPS

Try a new take on pork chops with this sweet and tangy recipe. Just a hint of mustard,
the sweet brown sugar and apples makes this recipe a regular go-to at our house.

**MAKES 4 TO 6 SERVINGS**

4 to 6 pork chops

2 green apples, sliced

1 small onion, diced

4 tbsp (60 ml) Dijon mustard

2 tbsp (28 g) brown sugar

Place the pork chops in the slow cooker. Slice the apples and add them to the slow cooker. Dice the onion into small pieces and add to the slow cooker. Add the Dijon mustard and brown sugar.

Cook on low for 6 to 8 hours or on high for 4 to 6 hours.

# MAPLE AND BROWN SUGAR HAM

Growing up I wasn't a huge ham lover; I'd always choose turkey instead. When I met my husband and learned of his love of ham, I had to find a recipe that we would both enjoy. This recipe adds a bit of sweet to the salty ham that's just the perfect balance of flavors and makes it a great recipe for the holidays.

**MAKES 6 TO 8 SERVINGS**

7 lb (3 kg) spiral-cut bone-in ham

1 cup (240 ml) water

1 cup (220 g) brown sugar

½ cup (118 ml) maple syrup

2 tbsp (30 ml) Dijon mustard

Place the ham in the slow cooker flat side down. Add water to the slow cooker. In a small-size bowl, mix together the brown sugar, maple syrup and mustard. Pour the mixture over the ham.

Cook on low for 4 hours. Baste the ham with the juices occasionally.

# BACON-WRAPPED PORK LOIN

My kids love bacon so it's always fun to find new ways to use it in our recipes. Wrapping a cut of meat like pork loin in bacon gives it a whole new delicious flavor that will have your family asking for seconds.

**MAKES 4 TO 6 SERVINGS**

3 to 4 lb (1.5 to 2.0 kg) pork loin

8 slices bacon

½ cup (110 g) brown sugar

2 tbsp (30 ml) Dijon mustard

2 tbsp (30 ml) honey

Wrap the pork loin in bacon. Place it in the slow cooker. In a medium-size bowl, mix together the brown sugar, Dijon mustard and honey. Coat the loin with the mixture, covering it completely.

Cook on low for 4 to 6 hours.

# DR. PEPPER PORK SANDWICHES

I'll be honest, I have a deep love for Dr. Pepper, and using it in these pork sandwiches is especially delicious. You can shred the pork and serve it on a bun or in a tortilla. I love that it has so many tasty options.

**MAKES 6 TO 8 SERVINGS**

2 lb (907 g) pork roast, shoulder or butt

12 oz (340 ml) Dr. Pepper

1 (18-oz [504-ml]) bottle BBQ sauce

1 tsp garlic powder

Buns, for serving

Place the pork roast in the slow cooker. Add the Dr. Pepper, BBQ sauce and garlic powder.

Cook on low for 6 to 8 hours or on high for 4 hours.

Serve on buns.

# SAUERKRAUT AND SAUSAGE

My dad and brother are huge sauerkraut lovers. I remember every year they would make it at least once for a family gathering. It's a great dinner option if you are in the mood to try something a little out of the ordinary.

**MAKES 4 TO 6 SERVINGS**

2 lb (907 g) sauerkraut

1 apple, sliced

¼ cup (55 g) brown sugar

1 sweet onion, diced

1 lb (454 g) kielbasa, sliced

Pour the sauerkraut into the slow cooker. Place the sliced apple in the slow cooker. Add the brown sugar, diced onion and sliced kielbasa.

Cook on low for 3 to 4 hours.

# HAM AND CHEESE POTATOES

One of the most delicious comfort food recipes to make is Ham and Cheese Potatoes. It's a recipe that's loaded with flavors and ingredients that will make you want to grab a bowl, cozy up to the table and enjoy this classic family favorite.

**MAKES 4 TO 6 SERVINGS**

8 to 10 large potatoes, peeled and diced

1 onion, diced

2 cups (300 g) ham, chopped

2 cups (241 g) cheddar cheese

1 (10-oz [283-g]) can cream of mushroom soup

1½ cups (355 ml) chicken broth

Salt and pepper

Add the potatoes, onion and ham to the slow cooker. Add the cheese, soup, broth and salt and pepper to taste.

Cook on low for 6 to 8 hours or on high for 4 hours. Remove the lid for the last 30 minutes.

# *Magnificent*
# MEATLESS
# MEALS

Meatless Monday is a day in our house when we try to make recipes without using any meat. Not only is this a great way to incorporate new forms of protein into our diet, but it also helps us when we're trying to stick to a budget. Here are some amazing meatless recipes you can use to start your own Meatless Monday tradition.

# QUINOA-STUFFED PEPPERS

Is there anything more delicious than a perfectly made stuffed pepper? You know, the kind that is loaded with salsa, beans and cheese and makes a great stand-alone meal option or even a side dish. Serving a meal in a pepper is so much fun, too—my boys love it!

**MAKES 8 SERVINGS**

4 green bell peppers

½ cup (93 g) quinoa, uncooked

1½ cups (260 g) salsa

1 (15-oz [425-g]) can black beans, drained and rinsed

1 cup (121 g) shredded cheddar cheese

Cut the peppers in half and use a spoon to scoop out the seeds. In a medium-size bowl, combine the quinoa, salsa, black beans and cheese. Fill the peppers with the mixture. Carefully place the peppers in the slow cooker.

Cook on low for 5 to 6 hours or on high for 3 to 4 hours.

# VEGETABLE SOUP

The soup no veggie lover can resist! The best part about vegetable soup is that you pick the veggies you want to add! This recipe includes our favorites, but you can easily personalize it to your taste.

**MAKES 6 TO 8 SERVINGS**

2 cups (289 g) frozen mixed vegetables

2 cups (289 g) frozen corn

4 (14.5-oz [411-g]) cans diced tomatoes

2 cups (473 ml) vegetable stock

1 onion, diced

2 cups (244 g) carrots, sliced

Homemade bread, for serving

Place all the ingredients in the slow cooker.

Cook on low for 4 to 6 hours.

Perfect served with homemade bread.

# BAKED POTATOES

Making baked potatoes in the slow cooker is not only incredibly convenient, but it is also a great way to cook them perfectly without drying them out. We like to have baked potato bars on Friday nights, where I place six potatoes in the slow cooker in the morning, and by suppertime they're ready. Offer all the fixings like butter, sour cream, cheese and even salsa for your family or guests to top their potatoes with.

### MAKES 6 SERVINGS

6 russet potatoes

Fixings (butter, sour cream, cheese or salsa), optional, for serving

Wash and dry the potatoes. Poke holes on all sides of the potatoes with a fork, and wrap them individually in aluminum foil. Place them in the slow cooker.

Cook on low for 6 to 8 hours.

Top with butter, sour cream, cheese or salsa.

# CORN ON THE COB

Warm, buttery corn on the cob makes the perfect side dish to any meal.

### MAKES 6 SERVINGS

6 ears corn, halved

1 cup (240 ml) milk

1 tbsp (10 g) garlic, minced

2 tbsp (29 g) butter

1 tsp salt

1 tsp pepper

Cut the ears of corn in half and place them in the slow cooker. Add all the other ingredients to the slow cooker.

Cook on low for 4 hours or on high for 2 hours.

# TEX-MEX QUINOA CASSEROLE

The taste of tacos without the meat, this zesty Tex-Mex dish will quickly become a vegetarian favorite!

**MAKES 6 TO 8 SERVINGS**

1 cup (170 g) quinoa, cooked

2 cups (473 ml) water

1 (10-oz [283-g]) can enchilada sauce

½ cup (72 g) corn

½ cup (100 g) black beans

½ cup (80 g) tomatoes, diced

1 (1-oz [28-g]) packet taco seasoning

2 cups (241 g) shredded cheese, plus more for serving

Fresh cilantro, for serving

Sour cream, for serving

In a medium-size saucepan, bring the quinoa and water to a boil. Reduce the heat to low, cover and simmer until tender and most of the liquid has been absorbed. Place the cooked quinoa in the slow cooker. Add the remaining ingredients.

Cook on low for 6 hours or on high for 4 hours.

Top with more cheese, fresh cilantro and sour cream!

# MINESTRONE SOUP

Classic minestrone soup has a tomato and vegetable broth base and is loaded to the max with fresh veggies, beans and tender pasta. Simmer with some spices and you have a delicious and healthy dinner!

**MAKES 6 TO 8 SERVINGS**

4 cups (946 ml) vegetable broth

2 cups (473 ml) water

2 onions, diced

2 cups (202 g) celery, chopped into bite-size pieces

2 cups (256 g) carrots, chopped into bite-size pieces

1 (14.5-oz [411-g]) can diced tomatoes

1 (15-oz [425-g]) can pinto beans

2 tbsp (20 g) garlic, minced

1 cup (90 g) ditalini pasta

2 tsp (1 g) basil

Salt and pepper, to taste

Pour the broth and water into the slow cooker. Add the onion, celery and carrots to the slow cooker. Add the remaining ingredients.

Cook on low for 6 to 8 hours or on high for 3 to 4 hours.

# CHEESE-STUFFED SHELLS

Stuffed shells feature classic Italian flavors like four different cheeses, garlic and red sauce. This Cheese-Stuffed Shells recipe is no exception, and it is creamy, cheesy and satisfying. With a side salad and warm garlic bread, this is perfect for a meatless family dinner!

**MAKES 5 TO 7 SERVINGS**

1 (24-oz [680-g]) jar pasta sauce

12 oz (340 g) ricotta cheese

1 cup (230 g) cottage cheese

2 cups (241 g) mozzarella cheese

1 egg

1 tbsp (8 g) Italian seasoning

½ cup (60 g) cheddar cheese, plus more for topping

10 to 15 pasta shells, cooked

Pour half of the pasta sauce in the slow cooker. Mix together the ricotta cheese, cottage cheese, mozzarella cheese, egg, Italian seasoning and cheddar cheese. Fill the cooked shells with the cheese mixture. Place the shells in the slow cooker. Top with the remaining pasta sauce, and sprinkle with cheddar cheese.

Cook on low for 3 hours.

# QUINOA CHILI

This delicious vegetarian take on chili has a little kick and a whole lot of flavor in it. Not only is it crazy easy, but it's absolutely delicious and good for you as well! It's packed with protein, nutrients and tons of flavor.

**MAKES 6 TO 8 SERVINGS**

1 cup (185 g) uncooked quinoa, rinsed

2 (28-oz [794-g]) cans diced tomatoes

2 (16-oz [454-g]) cans chili beans

3 cups (710 ml) vegetable stock

1 (15-oz [425-g]) can corn

2 tsp (6 g) chili powder

1 tsp garlic powder

1 tsp cumin

Add all of the ingredients to the slow cooker and stir to combine.

Cook on low for 6 to 8 hours or on high for 4 to 6 hours.

# Must-Make
# FISH AND
# SEAFOOD

In my house, we're huge seafood and fish lovers. Every year, we spend a week in Canada fishing with family. It's one of my favorite times of the year. Several of our fish and seafood recipes are now slow cooker favorites, and we wanted to share them with you!

# SHRIMP LOVER'S STEW

Loaded with shrimp, this mouthwatering stew is a seafood lover's dream!
We love to serve this delicious stew with cheesy biscuits and a side salad.

**MAKES 6 TO 8 SERVINGS**

1 lb (454 g) red potatoes, diced

1 (14.5-oz [411-g]) can diced tomatoes

4 cups (946 ml) vegetable broth

2 tbsp (20 g) garlic, minced

1 tsp cilantro

1 tsp basil

2 lb (907 g) large shrimp

Add the potatoes to the slow cooker with the diced tomatoes. Cover with the vegetable broth. Add the garlic, cilantro and basil.

Cook on low for 6 hours or on high for 2 to 3 hours.

Peel and devein the shrimp. Add the shrimp to the slow cooker 30 minutes before the dish is done.

# HONEY GARLIC SALMON

The most delicious way to enjoy salmon is with a sweet honey garlic glaze. This recipe cooks in just two short hours in the slow cooker, and paired with potatoes or a salad, it's the perfect meal.

**MAKES 4 TO 6 SERVINGS**

1 to 2 lb (454 to 907 g) salmon, skin on

½ cup (118 ml) honey

1 tbsp (10 g) garlic, minced

1 tbsp (15 ml) Worcestershire sauce

¼ cup (60 ml) soy sauce

Cover the bottom of the slow cooker with parchment paper. Place the salmon skin side down on the paper. In a small-size bowl, mix the honey, garlic, Worcestershire sauce and soy sauce together. Pour it over the salmon.

Cook on low for 2 hours.

# SHRIMP FAJITAS

Try this delicious seafood twist on a classic recipe. Serve these fajitas on tortillas with avocado and sour cream.

**MAKES 6 TO 8 SERVINGS**

1 green pepper, sliced

2 red peppers, sliced

1 onion, sliced

1 lb (454 g) mushrooms, sliced

2 tomatoes, quartered

1 lb (454 g) raw shrimp, deveined and peeled

1 cup (240 ml) chicken broth

1 (1-oz [28-g]) packet taco seasoning

1 tsp salt

Tortillas, for serving

Place all of the ingredients in the slow cooker.

Cook on low for 5 to 6 hours or on high for 3 to 4 hours.

Serve on tortillas.

# SHRIMP BOIL

When we're camping, we love to have crawfish and shrimp boils over the campfire.
It's something we look forward to in the summer months. This slow cooker Shrimp Boil
is incredibly similar, and we can easily make it year-round at home!

**MAKES 6 TO 8 SERVINGS**

1 lb (454 g) red potatoes

1 lemon, sliced

¼ cup (8 g) Old Bay seasoning

6 cups (1.5 L) water

1 lb (454 g) kielbasa sausage, cut

4 ears corn, cut into thirds

2 lb (907 g) shrimp

Place the potatoes, lemon, seasoning and water in the slow cooker. Cook on low for 3 hours.

Add the sausage and corn to the slow cooker. Cook on low for 2 hours.

Add the shrimp to the slow cooker. Cook on high for 30 minutes.

# SHRIMP JAMBALAYA

The first time I had Shrimp Jambalaya in Louisiana, I knew right away that I wanted to make this dish for my family. With its amazing flavor and just the right amount of spice, it's a seafood lover's dream.

**MAKES 6 TO 8 SERVINGS**

12 oz (340 g) smoked sausage (Any sausage will work great!)

1 onion, diced

1 tbsp (10 g) garlic, minced

2 (14-oz [392-g]) cans diced tomatoes

2 cups (480 ml) chicken broth

1 tsp oregano

1 green pepper, diced

1 lb (454 g) shrimp

1½ cups (315 g) rice

Place everything but the shrimp and rice in the slow cooker.

Cook on low for 4 to 6 hours.

Add the shrimp and rice 30 minutes before the dish is done. Fluff with a fork before serving.

Soups are a great dish to make in slow cookers. Traditional recipes like chili and stew are meals everyone loves to make. We've made slow cooker versions of some creamy soups that have been passed down in our family. You're going to love having a bowlful of comfort with these recipes!

# LOADED BAKED POTATO SOUP

I'll always remember my mom making potato soup when I was growing up. It was something
I looked forward to and ate way too much of! This loaded potato soup recipe is my take on Mom's recipe.
It's a delicious soup that's perfect to make on a cold winter day.

**MAKES 6 TO 8 SERVINGS**

4 cups (600 g) **russet potatoes**, diced

1 onion, chopped

4 cups (946 ml) chicken broth

½ cup (50 g) flour

4 tbsp (57 g) butter, melted

2 cups (470 g) **heavy cream**

½ cup (60 g) sour cream or yogurt

Chives, cheddar cheese, bacon,
for serving

Place the potatoes and onion in the slow cooker with the chicken broth.

Cook on low for 4 to 6 hours.

Make a roux by whisking the flour into the melted butter in a medium saucepan over medium heat. Add the heavy cream and sour cream. Add the roux to the slow cooker 30 minutes before the dish is done.

Top with chives, cheddar cheese and bacon.

# BROCCOLI-AND-CHEESE SOUP

I always order this when getting soup at a restaurant. There's just something about creamy broccoli soup that hits the spot. This is a cheesy soup even the kids will love!

**MAKES 6 TO 8 SERVINGS**

• • • • • • • • • • • • • • • • • • • • • • • • • • • • • • • • • • • • • • • • • • • • • • • •

1 (14-oz [396-g]) bag **frozen broccoli**

1 small onion, diced

1 (10-oz [284-g]) can **cream of mushroom soup**

1 cup (240 ml) chicken broth

1 (10-oz [284-g]) can **cream of chicken soup**

1 lb (454 g) **soft cheese** (I prefer Velveeta)

1 (5-oz [142-g]) can **evaporated milk**

Place all of the ingredients in the slow cooker. Stir occasionally.

Cook on low for 4 hours or on high for 2 hours.

# TOMATO BASIL SOUP

Creamy and rich Tomato Basil Soup made in the slow cooker—comfort food at its best! Serve this delicious soup topped with homemade croutons or a grilled cheese sandwich on the side.

**MAKES 6 TO 8 SERVINGS**

• • • • • • • • • • • • • • • • • • • • • • • • • • • • • • • • • • • • • • • • • • • • • • • •

4 cups (644 g) **tomatoes**, diced

4 cups (946 ml) chicken stock

2 tbsp (5 g) **basil**

1 cup (240 ml) **heavy cream**

12 oz (341 g) butter

Salt and pepper, to taste

Add all of the ingredients to the slow cooker.

Cook on low for 6 to 8 hours or on high for 4 to 6 hours. Use an immersion blender to purée before eating.

# CHICKEN AND POTATO STEW

Here's a wholesome stew that makes great leftovers. I love that this stew is made from ingredients that I always have on hand so I can put it together without much planning.

**MAKES 6 TO 8 SERVINGS**

- - - - - - - - - - - - - - - - - - - - - - - - - - - - - - - - - - - - - - - - - - - - - - - - - - - - - - - - - - - - - - -

5 **russet potatoes**, diced

5 cups (1 L) chicken broth

4 **chicken breasts**, cooked and shredded

1 (14.5-oz (411-g) can diced tomatoes

1 cup (128 g) carrots, diced

1 cup (101 g) **celery**, diced

1 tsp oregano

1 tsp garlic, minced

Salt and pepper, to taste

Add all of the ingredients to the slow cooker.

Cook on low for 7 to 8 hours or on high for 4 to 6 hours.

# BEEF AND NOODLE SOUP

Beef and Noodle Soup is a great twist on a traditional recipe. We like to serve this with a slice of homemade bread to soak up the broth.

**MAKES 6 TO 8 SERVINGS**

- - - - - - - - - - - - - - - - - - - - - - - - - - - - - - - - - - - - - - - - - - - - - - - - - - - - - - - - - - - - - - -

2 lb (907 g) **stew meat**

1 (1-oz [28-g]) packet **onion soup mix**

1 (10-oz [284-g]) can **cream of mushroom soup**

1 tbsp (10 g) garlic, minced

4 (14.5-oz [411-ml]) cans beef broth

1 (12-oz [340-g]) package **egg noodles**

Place everything but the noodles in the slow cooker.

Cook on low for 6 to 8 hours or on high for 4 to 6 hours.

Add the noodles 30 minutes before the dish is done. Adding the noodles last prevents them from getting mushy!

# CHICKEN TACO SOUP

This is a yummy, warming soup, thanks to the hearty and flavorful combination of chicken, vegetables and seasonings. Let your family or guests pick their toppings—my favorites are avocado, sour cream and tortilla chips!

**MAKES 6 TO 8 SERVINGS**

3 to 4 chicken breasts

4 cups (946 ml) chicken broth

1 (14.5-oz [411-g]) can diced tomatoes

1 onion, diced

1 tbsp (8 g) chili powder

1 (15-oz [425-g]) can black beans

2 cups (289 g) corn

¼ cup (4 g) fresh cilantro

Toppings (avocado, cheese, sour cream and tortilla chips), for serving

Add the chicken, chicken broth, tomatoes, onion and chili powder to the slow cooker.

Cook on low for 6 hours.

Remove the chicken and shred. Put it back in the slow cooker. Add the beans, corn and cilantro.

Cook on high for 30 minutes.

Serve with avocado, cheese, sour cream and tortilla chips.

# CHICKEN PARMESAN SOUP

Turn a classic entrée into a delicious soup. We love chicken Parmesan at our house. Chicken Parmesan Soup is a recipe that gets cooked over and over again!

**MAKES 6 TO 8 SERVINGS**

3 chicken breasts

2 (14.5-oz [411-g]) cans diced tomatoes

1 tbsp (10 g) garlic, minced

5 cups (1 L) chicken broth

1 onion, diced

1 cup (180 g) **Parmesan cheese**, plus more for serving

2 tsp (4 g) oregano

1 (8-oz [227-g]) box pasta

Add everything to the slow cooker but the pasta.

Cook on low for 6 to 8 hours or on high for 3 to 4 hours.

Shred the chicken and add the pasta 30 minutes before the dish is done. Top with extra cheese.

# MUSHROOM SOUP

Mushroom lovers will not be able to get enough of this hearty and delicious soup!
For a fun twist, try adding ¼ cup (60 ml) of Marsala wine!

**MAKES 6 TO 8 SERVINGS**

1 tbsp (14 g) butter

1 lb (454 g) **mushrooms**, sliced

1 medium onion, diced

4 cups (946 ml) chicken broth

2 tbsp (17 g) flour

1 cup (121 g) sour cream

1 cup (240 ml) **heavy cream**

Salt and pepper

In a large-size skillet over medium heat, melt the butter and sauté the mushrooms and onion for 5 minutes. Place them in the slow cooker with the chicken broth.

Cook on low for 6 hours.

Add the flour, sour cream and heavy cream. Cook on high for an additional 30 minutes. Add salt and pepper to taste.

# FRENCH ONION SOUP →

If you're a fan of French Onion Soup, this will easily become your go-to recipe—it's so simple and delicious!
This is also a great recipe to use as a dip for warm roast beef sandwiches.

**MAKES 6 TO 8 SERVINGS**

4 large onions, sliced

4 tbsp (57 g) butter

6 cups (1.5 L) beef broth

¼ cup (60 ml) dry sherry cooking wine

1 tsp **soy sauce**

1½ cups (270 g) **Parmesan cheese**

Place the sliced onions in the slow cooker. Add the butter, broth, wine and soy sauce.

Cook on low for 2 to 3 hours.

Add the Parmesan cheese 30 minutes before the dish is done.

# EASY CHILI

One of our favorite recipes to make in the slow cooker has always been a hearty chili. Making great chili has
never been so simple with this easy recipe! Top with sour cream and shredded cheese for a tasty meal.

**MAKES 6 TO 8 SERVINGS**

1 lb (454 g) **ground beef**

1 lb (454 g) **sausage**

2 (14.5-oz [411-g]) cans diced tomatoes

2 (14.5-oz [411-g]) cans **tomato sauce**

2 (16-oz [454-g]) cans **chili beans**

2 tbsp (17 g) chili powder

1 tbsp (10 g) garlic, minced

1 onion, diced

**Toppings** (sour cream, shredded cheese)

In a large-size skillet, cook the beef over medium heat for 8 to 10 minutes or until brown
and place it in the slow cooker. Cook the sausage for 8 to 10 minutes or until brown and
place it in the slow cooker. Add the tomatoes, tomato sauce, beans, chili powder, garlic
and onion.

Cook on low for 4 to 6 hours.

Top with your choice of toppings and enjoy.

# CLAM CHOWDER

We like making Clam Chowder on Christmas Eve. It's a recipe that has become a Christmas family tradition. This slow cooker Clam Chowder is not only simple to make, but the flavors are great, too.

**MAKES 6 TO 8 SERVINGS**

3 russet potatoes, diced

1 onion, diced

3 (6-oz [170-g]) cans chopped clams

1 (8-oz [237-ml]) bottle clam juice

2 tbsp (29 g) butter

3 tbsp (23 g) flour

1 cup (240 ml) milk

1 cup (240 ml) half-and-half

Toppings (oyster crackers, bacon), optional, for serving

Place the potatoes, onion, clams and clam juice in the slow cooker.

Cook on low for 6 hours or on high for 4 hours.

Melt the butter in a small saucepan and add the flour until bubbly, about 5 minutes. Add the milk and half-and-half until it's smooth, about 5 minutes. Add this to the slow cooker and continue to cook on low for 30 minutes.

Serve with oyster crackers or top with bacon.

# BACON CHEESEBURGER SOUP

Adding a dish like Bacon Cheeseburger Soup to our meal rotation has been a huge win for our family. My kids love the combination of burger, cheese and potatoes all in one delicious bowl.

**MAKES 6 TO 8 SERVINGS**

1 lb (454 g) ground beef

1 onion, diced

1 cup (110 g) carrots, shredded

3 tbsp (43 g) butter, divided

4 cups (600 g) potatoes, diced

4 cups (946 g) chicken broth

2 tsp (3 g) Italian seasoning

½ lb (227 g) bacon, cooked and crumbled

¼ cup (31 g) flour

3 cups (362 g) shredded cheddar cheese

1½ cups (355 ml) milk

¼ cup (30 g) sour cream

Salt and pepper

In a large-size skillet, cook the beef over medium heat for 8 to 10 minutes or until brown and place it in the slow cooker. Sauté the onion and carrots in 1 tablespoon (14 g) of butter and add to the slow cooker. Add the potatoes, broth, seasoning and bacon to the slow cooker.

Cook on low for 4 to 6 hours.

Thirty minutes before the dish is done, melt 2 tablespoons (29 g) of butter in a small-size saucepan and add the flour. Cook until bubbly, about 5 minutes. Add it to the slow cooker—this will help thicken the soup. Add the cheese, milk, sour cream and salt and pepper to taste.

# Recipes Worth
# WAKING UP
# FOR

My absolute favorite meal of the day is breakfast. I love nothing more than waking up to eggs, French toast and all those other delicious breakfast foods waiting for me in the slow cooker. These breakfast recipes can be put in the slow cooker on low the night before and will be ready to eat in the morning.

# BLUEBERRY FRENCH TOAST CASSEROLE

I love making this dish for Christmas morning brunch. I start it right when we get up, and it's ready to eat after my kids have opened gifts and family has arrived! With fresh blueberries in a sweet, breaded casserole, this delicious dish will taste like you spent hours in the kitchen!

**MAKES 6 TO 8 SERVINGS**

1 loaf French bread

6 eggs, beaten

2 cups (473 ml) milk

⅔ cup (128 g) sugar

1 tbsp (15 ml) vanilla

4 cups (606 g) blueberries

Sugar, whipped cream, for serving

Cut the French bread into cubes and place them in the slow cooker. In a medium-size bowl, whisk together the eggs, milk, sugar and vanilla. Fold in the blueberries. Pour the mixture over the bread. Mix slightly. Place a layer of paper towels under the lid to catch any condensation.

Cook on high for 2 to 3 hours.

Top with sugar and whipped cream.

# BREAKFAST POTATOES

You can't have breakfast without a side of potatoes, and this recipe hits the spot! These yummy potatoes make a great add-on to any brunch menu. You're sure to impress your family or guests with these.

**MAKES 6 TO 8 SERVINGS**

1 (30-oz [851-g]) package hash browns

1 onion, diced

1 green bell pepper, diced

12 oz (340 g) sausage, sliced

1½ cups (181 g) shredded cheddar cheese

½ cup (60 g) sour cream

1 (10-oz [284-g]) can cream of chicken soup

1 tbsp (10 g) garlic, minced

Salt and pepper

Place the hash browns in the slow cooker. Add the onion, pepper and sausage to the slow cooker. In a medium-size bowl, mix the cheese, sour cream, soup and garlic. Pour it over the hash browns. Add salt and pepper to taste.

Cook on low for 6 hours or on high for 4 hours.

# HOMEMADE GRANOLA ⊙

This is the perfect addition to your favorite yogurt or oatmeal! It's tasty enough to eat by the handful on its own, too, making it the perfect after-school snack. Save money by making your own granola!

**MAKES 8 TO 10 SERVINGS**

. . . . . . . . . . . . . . . . . . . . . . . . . . . . . . . . . . . . . . . . . . . . . . . . . .

5 cups (402 g) oatmeal

½ cup (43 g) sliced almonds

1 cup (151 g) raisins

1 cup (240 ml) honey

½ cup (90 g) peanut butter

½ cup (115 g) butter

2 tsp (5 g) cinnamon

1 tbsp (15 ml) vanilla

Spray the slow cooker with a nonstick cooking spray. Add the oatmeal, almonds and raisins. In a medium-size bowl, melt the honey, peanut butter and butter in the microwave for 45 seconds and mix together. Pour the mixture into the slow cooker. Add the cinnamon and vanilla.

Cook on low for 4 hours or on high for 2 hours. Stir every 30 minutes.

# CARAMEL APPLE OATMEAL

There isn't a better way to start the day than with a bowl of hot oatmeal! This could also be an easy weeknight dessert. Serve it warm with a dollop of whipped cream or a scoop of vanilla ice cream!

**MAKES 6 TO 8 SERVINGS**

. . . . . . . . . . . . . . . . . . . . . . . . . . . . . . . . . . . . . . . . . . . . . . . . . .

1 cup (80 g) steel-cut oatmeal

4 cups (946 ml) milk

2 apples, chopped

1 tsp cinnamon

4 tbsp (60 ml) maple syrup

Place all of the ingredients in the slow cooker. Gently stir together.

Cook on low for 8 hours or on high for 4 hours.

# VEGGIE FRITTATA

Packed with delicious vegetables, this frittata is the perfect breakfast, brunch or quick weeknight dinner for veggie lovers! The delicious flavors of the mushrooms, tomatoes, green peppers, garlic and cheese blend together perfectly.

**MAKES 6 TO 8 SERVINGS**

1 cup (30 g) fresh baby spinach

1 cup (59 g) mushrooms, sliced

1 cup (161 g) tomatoes, diced

½ cup (75 g) green pepper, diced

1 tbsp (10 g) garlic, minced

6 eggs

½ cup (118 ml) milk

1 tsp seasoning salt

1 cup (121 g) cheddar cheese

Sour cream, fresh parsley, green onions, optional, for serving

Spray the slow cooker generously. Place the veggies and garlic in the bottom of the slow cooker. Mix together the eggs, milk and seasoning salt. Pour the mixture over the veggies in the slow cooker.

Cook on high for 2½ hours. Add the cheese 15 minutes before the cooking is done.

Cut into wedges and top with sour cream, fresh parsley and green onions.

# CINNAMON ROLL CASSEROLE ○

Enjoy warm, fresh cinnamon rolls straight out of your slow cooker with this recipe! Indulge your brunch guests with this rich, fluffy Cinnamon Roll Casserole made from simple ingredients you're likely to have on hand.

**MAKES 6 TO 8 SERVINGS**

2 tubes refrigerated cinnamon rolls

½ cup (118 ml) butter, melted

½ cup (100 g) brown sugar

1 tsp cinnamon

Quarter each cinnamon roll. Place a layer in a greased slow cooker. Mix together the butter, sugar and cinnamon. Pour it over the cinnamon rolls. Place a second layer of cinnamon rolls on top.

Cook on low for 4 hours or on high for 2 hours.

Spread icing on top!

# BACON BREAKFAST CASSEROLE

If you love bacon, you are going to love this casserole! This cheesy egg casserole with cooked crumbled bacon, diced onion and hash browns is sure to be a crowd-pleaser at breakfast or brunch!

**MAKES 6 TO 8 SERVINGS**

1 (30-oz [851-g]) bag hash browns

12 eggs

½ cup (118 ml) milk

1 onion, diced

1 lb (454 g) bacon, cooked and crumbled

1 cup (121 g) cheddar cheese, shredded, plus more for topping

1 cup (121 g) mozzarella cheese, shredded, plus more for topping

Spray the slow cooker with nonstick cooking spray. Layer half of the hash browns on the bottom of the slow cooker. Whisk the eggs, milk, onion, bacon and cheese. Pour the mixture over the hash browns. Top with extra cheese.

Cook on low for 8 hours or on high for 4 hours.

Cook this overnight and you'll have breakfast ready in the morning!

Tasty

# APPETIZERS
# AND SIDES

Impress your party guests with these tasty appetizers and easy sides. Instead of being stuck in the kitchen preparing all the food, you'll be able to spend more time enjoying your guests by making these simple recipes.

# SWEET PARTY MEATBALLS

Delight guests with juicy meatballs smothered in a sweet honey BBQ sauce! They're great as a main dish but can also be used as an appetizer. Or they can even be made into a meatball sub with a slice of your favorite cheese to top them off.

**MAKES 10 TO 12 SERVINGS**

1 (26-oz [737-g]) package frozen meatballs

1½ cups (355 ml) BBQ sauce

12 oz (354 ml) chili sauce

1 cup (240 ml) honey

1 tsp garlic powder

1 tsp onion powder

Place the meatballs in the slow cooker. In a large-size bowl, combine the BBQ sauce, chili sauce, honey, garlic powder and onion powder. Pour the mixture over the meatballs.

Cook on low for 6 hours or on high for 4 hours.

# APPLE BBQ SAUSAGE BITES

Little smokies just got even better with this recipe! A sweet, tangy and spicy sauce coats these little smoked sausages. This makes a great appetizer for parties or a main dish for the hot dog lovers in your family (I'm looking at you, kids.)

**MAKES 10 TO 12 SERVINGS**

1 (14-oz [397-g]) package little smokies

1 cup (240 ml) applesauce

1 cup (240 ml) BBQ sauce

3 tsp (15 ml) Worcestershire sauce

½ cup (110 g) brown sugar

1 tsp garlic powder

Place the little smokies in the slow cooker. In a medium-size bowl, combine the applesauce, BBQ sauce, Worcestershire, brown sugar and garlic powder. Pour the mixture over the little sausages.

Cook on low for 6 hours or on high for 4 hours.

# PIZZA DIP

Easy to prepare, and who doesn't like pizza? This is a great dip for parties or as a snack for the whole family. Serve with pita bread chips, crackers or even a thinly sliced baguette. Enjoy the taste of pizza in every bite!

MAKES 10 TO 12 SERVINGS

1 (8-oz [227-g]) cream cheese

1 cup (240 ml) pizza sauce

1 cup (120 g) pepperoni

1 cup (66 g) mushrooms, sliced

¼ cup (45 g) green olives

¼ cup (45 g) black olives

Crackers (I prefer Ritz), for serving

Place the cream cheese, pizza sauce and pepperoni in the slow cooker. Add the sliced mushrooms, green olives and black olives to the slow cooker.

Cook on low for 4 to 6 hours or on high for 2 to 3 hours.

Use crackers for dipping.

# CINNAMON ROASTED ALMONDS

Covered in a sugary cinnamon coating, these almonds are the perfect treat to snack on. Sweet almonds with a hint of cinnamon make for an easy and delicious gift for the holidays, too. You'll have to limit yourself with these, or you'll find yourself eating way more than you planned!

MAKES 10 TO 12 SERVINGS

3 cups (511 g) almonds, whole and raw

1½ cups (288 g) sugar

3 tbsp (23 g) cinnamon

2 tsp (10 ml) vanilla

1 egg white

Place the almonds in the slow cooker. In a medium-size bowl, combine the sugar, cinnamon, vanilla and egg white. Pour the mixture over the almonds. Gently stir so that the almonds are well coated in the mixture.

Cook on low for 4 hours or on high for 2 hours. Stir every 20 minutes.

# HAMBURGER NACHO DIP

This awesome cheesy dip is a definite crowd-pleaser! Kick it up a notch by using a jar of your favorite salsa in place of the diced tomatoes. If you like spicy salsa, this will really turn up the flavor. Hamburger Nacho Dip is a cheesy and addictive treat!

**MAKES 10 TO 12 SERVINGS**

. . . . . . . . . . . . . . . . . . . . . . . . . . . . . . . . . . . . . . . . . . . . . . . . . . . . . . . . . . .

1 lb (454 g) ground beef

1 (32-oz [907-g]) package soft cheese (I prefer Velveeta)

1 (10-oz [283-g]) can diced tomatoes

1 (10.5-oz [298-g]) can cream of mushroom soup

Chips or vegetables, optional, for serving

In a skillet, cook the hamburger on medium heat for 8 to 10 minutes or until browned. Place it in the slow cooker. Add the remaining ingredients to the slow cooker.

Cook on low for 6 to 8 hours or on high for 4 hours.

Serve with chips or veggies.

*Note:*

If you're short on time, you can place the ground beef in the slow cooker without browning. Simply follow all the other steps in the recipe the same way. The texture of the recipe may be slightly altered with this change, but it will still be delicious!

# BUFFALO CHICKEN DIP

This creamy and spicy dip makes the perfect game-day appetizer! Five simple ingredients in your slow cooker make this creamy, cheesy and zesty hot dip taste just like Buffalo wings. You'll win with this crowd-pleasing dish!

**MAKES 10 TO 12 SERVINGS**

2 chicken breasts

4 oz (113 g) cream cheese

½ cup (60 g) sour cream

1 cup (240 ml) hot sauce

4 oz (113 g) blue cheese, crumbled

Chips or vegetables, optional, for serving

Place the chicken in the slow cooker. In a medium-size bowl, combine the cream cheese, sour cream, hot sauce and blue cheese. Pour the mixture over the chicken.

Cook on low for 4 hours or on high for 2 hours. Shred the chicken with a fork.

Serve with chips or veggies.

# MASHED CAULIFLOWER

This recipe is a delicious alternative to mashed potatoes you definitely have to try for yourself! You'll get a whole lot of flavor without all the guilt. Best of all, most of the time you'll have the ingredients on hand, so it's a win-win!

**MAKES 6 TO 8 SERVINGS**

1 lb (454 g) cauliflower

2 tbsp (28 g) garlic, minced

1 cup (180 g) Parmesan cheese, shredded

2 tbsp (29 g) butter

Salt

Place the cauliflower in the slow cooker. Add the garlic. Pour enough water in the slow cooker to cover the cauliflower.

Cook on low for 6 hours.

Drain the excess water. Place the cauliflower back in the slow cooker. Add the cheese, butter and salt to taste.

Mash with a potato masher and serve.

# REFRIED BEANS

These smooth and creamy beans make a tasty side dish for tacos. They taste like they came from your favorite Mexican restaurant, and they're so easy to make. Even the pickiest eaters love this recipe!

**MAKES 8 TO 10 SERVINGS**

½ lb (227 g) pinto beans

½ lb (227 g) black beans

1 onion, shredded

2 tbsp (20 g) garlic, minced

1 tbsp (8 g) cumin

7 cups (1.7 L) water

Place all of the ingredients in the slow cooker.

Cook on low for 8 to 10 hours. Use an immersion blender or potato masher to mash.

# GARLIC PARMESAN MUSHROOMS

These rich and flavorful mushrooms are great as a side, on top of meat or by themselves.
Anyone who loves mushrooms will ask for these tender mushrooms time and time again.
If you have leftovers, you could slice them as a topping for your pizza!

**MAKES 6 TO 8 SERVINGS**

2 lb (907 g) mushrooms

1 cup (240 ml) vegetable stock

¼ cup (60 ml) half-and-half

1 cup (230 g) butter

1 (1-oz [28-g]) packet ranch dressing mix

½ cup (90 g) Parmesan cheese, shredded

Wash and clean the mushrooms. Place the mushrooms in the slow cooker with the vegetable stock.

Cook on low for 4 hours.

Mix the half-and-half, butter, ranch mix and Parmesan, and add it to the slow cooker 30 minutes before serving.

# PULL-APART BREAD

A savory version of monkey bread, this tasty and easy appetizer is perfect for any occasion. Pull-Apart Bread is a great side dish to pizza, lasagna and spaghetti, to name a few. Your family will love this bread!

**MAKES 8 TO 10 SERVINGS**

1 tsp garlic salt

1 tsp Italian seasoning

1 cup (180 g) Parmesan cheese

1 (16.3-oz [462-g]) can refrigerated biscuits (I prefer large Grands)

½ cup (115 g) butter

Spray the slow cooker with a nonstick spray.

Combine the garlic salt, seasoning and Parmesan cheese in a Ziploc bag. Separate the biscuits, and add them to the bag. Shake the bag until the biscuits are covered in the seasoning mixture. Remove the biscuits from the bag and place them in the slow cooker. Top with butter.

Cook on low for 2 to 3 hours.

# CANDIED SWEET POTATOES

Typically served as a traditional Thanksgiving dish, these sweet, buttery yams are a perfect side dish to any dinner! They are easy to make and if you bring them to Thanksgiving, chances are you will be asked to bring them again.

**MAKES 8 TO 10 SERVINGS**

2 (29-oz [822-g]) cans yams

½ cup (115 g) butter

2 tbsp (24 g) sugar

2 eggs

½ cup (118 ml) milk

1 cup (220 g) plus 2 tbsp (28 g) brown sugar, divided

1 cup (121 g) pecans, diced

½ cup (118 ml) butter, melted

½ cup (50 g) flour

1 tsp vanilla

Spread the yams on the bottom of the slow cooker and arrange pats of butter on top of them. Sprinkle the sugar over the butter. In a medium-size bowl, combine the eggs and milk. Pour the mixture on top. Sprinkle 2 tablespoons (28 g) of brown sugar over the mixture.

For the topping, combine the pecans, 1 cup (220 g) of brown sugar, butter, flour and vanilla in a medium-size bowl. Pour the mixture on top of the yams.

Cook on low for 4 to 6 hours or on high for 2 hours.

# BROWN SUGAR-CINNAMON GLAZED CARROTS

Carrots that are sweet, savory and simply amazing make for a flavorful and easy side dish for any weeknight meal. If your family is like ours, eating vegetables is always a top concern. Your kids won't even think of these as vegetables!

**MAKES 8 TO 10 SERVINGS**

6 cups (840 g) baby carrots

2 tbsp (29 g) butter

½ cup (110 g) brown sugar

2 tsp (5 g) cinnamon

Dash of salt

Place all of the ingredients in the slow cooker.

Cook on low for 6 to 8 hours or on high for 3 to 4 hours.

# MOM'S BAKED BEANS

Nobody's recipe can beat Mom's recipe! These yummy baked beans are the best, hands down. The saltiness of the bacon combined with the sweet flavor twist of the pineapple will keep you wanting more.

1 lb (454 g) bacon

1 onion, chopped

4 (15-oz [425-g]) cans pork and beans

1 (20-oz [567-g]) can crushed pineapple, drained

¼ cup (60 ml) ketchup

⅛ cup (30 ml) mustard

1 cup (220 g) brown sugar

In a large-size skillet, cook the bacon on medium-low heat for 5 minutes or until crispy. Cut the bacon into bite-size pieces and place them in the slow cooker. Add the remaining ingredients to the slow cooker.

Cook on low for 6 to 8 hours or on high for 4 hours.

For the last hour of cooking, slightly tip the lid of the slow cooker to help the sauce thicken.

# CORN CASSEROLE

If you like corn and love warm bread, this is the casserole for you! I always make it when we have chili. The cream cheese and creamed corn makes it nice and moist. This is a great side dish to bring to a family gathering since it really goes well with any meal.

**MAKES 8 TO 10 SERVINGS**

1 (8-oz [227-g]) box corn muffin mix

1 (8-oz [227-g]) tub cream cheese

2 cups (289 g) corn

1 (14-oz [397-g]) can creamed corn

½ cup (96 g) sugar

2 tbsp (29 g) butter

Salt and pepper, to taste

Place all of the ingredients in the slow cooker.

Cook on low for 6 hours or on high for 2 to 4 hours. Stir occasionally.

# MASHED POTATOES

Enjoy fluffy mashed potatoes packed full of flavor to go along with dinner. These store in the fridge and warm up as delicious as when you first cooked them. Add a vegetable and protein, and you are set for a meal!

**MAKES 8 TO 10 SERVINGS**

4 lb (1.8 kg) potatoes

½ cup (118 ml) chicken broth

2 tbsp (20 g) garlic, minced

1 cup (121 g) sour cream

½ cup (115 g) butter

4 oz (113 g) cream cheese

Peel and cut the potatoes into chunks. Place the potatoes in the slow cooker and add the chicken broth.

Cook on low for 4 hours.

Add the garlic, sour cream, butter and cream cheese. Mix together and serve.

# GREEN BEAN CASSEROLE

Whether you are making it for a holiday or just a dinner at home, this traditional Thanksgiving side dish is always a big hit! Delicious and easy to make, these green beans in a creamy white sauce always warm up a meal. The can't-miss french fried onion topping gives a crunch that makes you crave another bite!

### MAKES 8 TO 10 SERVINGS

3 (10.75-oz [305-g]) cans cream of mushroom soup

½ cup (118 ml) milk

⅛ tsp salt

⅛ tsp black pepper

1 lb (454 g) fresh mushrooms

10 (14.5-oz [411-g]) cans cut green beans, drained

2 (6-oz [170-g]) canisters french fried onions, divided

½ cup (60 g) shredded cheddar cheese

Pour the cream of mushroom soup, milk, salt and pepper into the slow cooker and mix together. Cut the mushrooms into slices, and add them to the slow cooker with the green beans and mix together. Add 1 canister of fried onions. Carefully mix everything together.

Cook on low for 4 to 6 hours or on high 2 to 4 hours.

Top with the second can of fried onions 30 minutes before the dish is done.

Top with the shredded cheddar cheese to give a new twist on an old favorite.

# Simple & Sweet

# DESSERTS

Who knew you could make dessert in a slow cooker? Everything from sweet cherry crisp to a gooey fudgy brownie can be waiting for you after a day of work when you put just a few ingredients in your slow cooker. Find a simple sweet treat in this chapter with some of my favorite desserts!

# CHERRY CRISP ➡

A mixture of sweet and tart, this traditional dessert is deliciously simple and an easy dessert to make for company. Every time I serve this, I remember I need to keep this on my quick "what to make or bring" list!

### MAKES 8 TO 10 SERVINGS

. . . . . . . . . . . . . . . . . . . . . . . . . . . . . . . . . . . . . . . . . . . . . . .

2 (21-oz [595-g]) cans cherry pie filling

1 (15.25-oz [432-g]) box yellow cake mix

½ cup (118 ml) melted butter

Nuts, optional, for serving

Pour the pie filling into the slow cooker. In a medium-size bowl, mix the cake mix together with the butter and add it to the slow cooker.

Cook on low for 4 to 6 hours. Top with nuts if desired.

# CINNAMON AND BROWN SUGAR APPLES

A combination of sweet cinnamon and fresh apples makes this dessert one you'll want to enjoy again soon! This is a perfect sweet side dish for a chilly night, or you can serve it with peanut butter toast as a topping for an after-school snack or breakfast!

### MAKES 8 TO 10 SERVINGS

. . . . . . . . . . . . . . . . . . . . . . . . . . . . . . . . . . . . . . . . . . . . . . .

6 to 8 honey crisp apples, sliced

½ cup (110 g) brown sugar

½ cup (96 g) granulated sugar

2 tsp (5 g) cinnamon

1 tsp nutmeg

Pinch of salt

3 tbsp (28 g) cornstarch

3 tbsp (43 g) unsalted butter

In a medium-size bowl, stir the apples together with the brown sugar, granulated sugar, cinnamon, nutmeg, salt and cornstarch until the apples are well coated. Cut the butter into small cubes and mix them into the apple and sugar mixture. Pour it into the slow cooker.

Cook on low for 4 hours.

This will turn mushy quickly if it's cooked longer, so keep an eye on the clock!

# S'MORES
# HOT FUDGE CAKE

The best thing about the great outdoors are s'mores! Now you can get them any time with this yummy recipe that features a rich, chocolatey cake paired with gooey hot fudge, crushed graham crackers and melted marshmallows!

**MAKES 8 TO 10 SERVINGS**

1½ cups (135 g) crushed graham crackers

½ cup (96 g) sugar

6 tbsp (89 ml) butter, melted

1 (15-oz [425-g]) box chocolate cake mix

1 (11.5-oz [326-g]) bag milk chocolate chips

2 cups (99 g) mini marshmallows

Spray the slow cooker with nonstick cooking spray.

Mix the graham crackers, sugar and butter. Pour the mixture into the slow cooker. Prepare the chocolate cake mix according to the instructions on the box. Pour it into the slow cooker.

Cook on low for 2 to 3 hours.

Top with the chocolate chips and marshmallows 30 minutes before the dish is done.

Crushed Golden Grahams cereal works great in replacement of graham crackers!

# FUDGY BROWNIES

Get chocolate heaven in just a few hours. You'll want more than one helping of this amazing dessert!
This is a popular recipe and easy to toss together in the slow cooker.

**MAKES 8 TO 10 SERVINGS**

1 (15-oz [425-g]) box brownie mix

1 cup (180 g) chocolate chips

⅔ cup (158 ml) oil

¼ cup (60 ml) water

2 eggs

1 (3.4-oz [96-g]) box instant pudding

2 cups (473 ml) milk

In a medium-size bowl, mix the brownie mix, chocolate chips, oil, water and eggs together. Pour the mixture into the slow cooker.

In a small-size bowl, mix the pudding mix and milk together. Pour it into the slow cooker and let sit; do not mix it with the brownie mixture.

Cook on low for 2 to 3 hours.

Serve with ice cream.

# STUFFED APPLES

Juicy apples stuffed with a sweet filling will put this dessert on everyone's favorite list! The holidays are full of heavy desserts, but this dessert is perfect if you want something a little bit lighter. If you aren't a crust lover, this Stuffed Apple is for you!

**MAKES 8 TO 10 SERVINGS**

2 tbsp (30 ml) butter, melted

2 tbsp (24 g) sugar

½ cup (60 g) pecans

1 tsp cinnamon

½ cup (40 g) oatmeal

½ cup (118 ml) apple juice

6 apples, cored

In a medium-size bowl, combine the butter, sugar, pecans, cinnamon and oatmeal. Pour the apple juice in the slow cooker. Add the cored apples and fill each one with the oatmeal mixture.

Cook on low for 4 to 6 hours or on high for 2 to 3 hours.

# APPLE PEAR BUTTER

Apple Pear Butter is a delicious fruit spread. If you're ready to change up your normal butter spread, try this out! Serve it with warm biscuits or scones for a sweet topping.

**MAKES 20 SERVINGS**

5 apples, peeled and sliced

3 pears, peeled and sliced

1 (50-oz [1.4-kg]) jar unsweetened applesauce

2 cups (383 g) sugar

1 tsp cinnamon

Place the apple and pear slices in the slow cooker. Add the applesauce, sugar and cinnamon.

Cook on low for 8 to 10 hours. Stir occasionally.

# CHOCOLATE FUDGE SAUCE ➡

This rich chocolate sauce is the perfect topping to take any dessert from average to amazing!
Classic hot fudge sauce drizzled over cheesecake will keep you coming back for more.
I like to use it for kids' parties on an ice cream bar as well.

**MAKES 10 TO 12 SERVINGS**

1 (11.5-oz [326-g]) bag milk chocolate chips

1 (11.5-oz [326-g]) bag semisweet chocolate chips

1 cup (240 ml) heavy cream

½ cup (118 ml) milk

2 tbsp (29 g) butter

1 tsp vanilla

Add all of the ingredients to the slow cooker and mix together.

Cook on low for 2 hours. Stir occasionally.

This chocolate sauce is great to use as fondue with fruit, cookies, angel food cake and more!

# CARAMEL SAUCE

Drizzle this rich sauce over ice cream or fresh apples. You could even drizzle it over bread pudding. A perfect one-ingredient topping for any dessert is a complete win in my book!

**MAKES 10 TO 12 SERVINGS**

2 to 4 (14-oz [396-g]) cans sweetened condensed milk

Mason jars

Divide the sweetened condensed milk into mason jars and seal the lids onto the jars. Place the jars in the slow cooker. Fill the slow cooker with water until the jars are completely submerged—this will keep the caramel from scorching in the slow cooker.

Cook on low for 8 hours.

SAUCES

*in a Snap*

Did you know you can make everything from fresh salsa to Alfredo sauce in the slow cooker? It's a great way to make a large batch of these favorite sauces to use now or freeze and use later. You'll be amazed how cooking low and slow in the slow cooker really gives these sauces amazing flavor.

# FRESH SALSA

Loaded with flavor and spice, this salsa is irresistible! This all-purpose salsa is great on tortilla chips, tacos and other Mexican-style favorites. The jalapeño peppers give the salsa an excellent flavor.

**MAKES 20 SERVINGS**

8 cups (1.3 kg) red tomatoes, diced

2 onions, diced

1 green pepper, diced

1 jalapeño pepper, diced

2 tsp (4 g) fresh cilantro

2 tsp (10 g) salt

Add the tomatoes, onions and peppers to the slow cooker, then add the cilantro and salt.

Cook on low for 4 to 5 hours or on high for 3 to 4 hours.

You can easily freeze salsa in a freezer bag or use a hot water bath to can.

# ⊙ SPAGHETTI SAUCE

Make delicious homemade spaghetti sauce without the hassle of spending all day in the kitchen! It took all summer to grow your tomatoes, now use a slow cooker to make them into a versatile tomato sauce. All you need to do is to add some cooked spaghetti noodles to your sauce, and you're set for mealtime!

**MAKES 6 TO 8 SERVINGS**

1 lb (454 g) ground beef

2 (14.5-oz [411-g]) cans diced tomatoes

2 (15-oz [425 g]) cans tomato sauce

1 tsp garlic salt

1 tsp oregano

1 tsp red pepper

In a medium-size skillet, cook the beef on medium heat for 8 to 10 minutes or until the meat is brown. Place it in the slow cooker. Add the rest of the ingredients to the slow cooker. Stir occasionally.

Cook on low for 8 to 10 hours or on high for 6 to 8 hours.

# MARINARA SAUCE

A zesty marinara sauce that will add the flavor you've been looking for to multiple dishes like my favorite lasagna! This is a simple tomato sauce with garlic, onion and oregano. Those flavors welcome any of your favorite pastas or meatballs to join the sauce!

**MAKES 6 TO 8 SERVINGS**

2 (28–oz [794-g]) cans crushed tomatoes

1 (16-oz [454-g]) can tomato paste

1 small onion, diced

2 tbsp (20 g) garlic, minced

1 tsp salt

2 tbsp (6 g) oregano

Add all of the ingredients to the slow cooker. Stir occasionally.

Cook on low for 4 to 6 hours.

# BLUEBERRY JAM ➜

Add the delicious flavor of blueberries to toast, bagels, pancakes and more with this great jam.
Quick prep work makes for an easy jam. With only four ingredients, this is the way to go!

**MAKES 20 SERVINGS**

. . . . . . . . . . . . . . . . . . . . . . . . . . . . . . . . . . . . . . . . . . . . . . . . . . . . .

2 lb (907 g) blueberries

1 cup (192 g) sugar

2 tsp (5 g) cinnamon

1 tsp lemon juice

Place all of the ingredients in the slow cooker. Stir occasionally.

Cook on low for 5 to 6 hours or on high for 3 to 4 hours.

# GARLIC ALFREDO SAUCE

This creamy, luscious Alfredo sauce with a hint of garlic will have everyone going back for seconds!
It turns a busy weeknight dinner into something special. Serve it with fettuccine,
or pour it over chicken breasts or steamed vegetables.

**MAKES 6 TO 8 SERVINGS**

. . . . . . . . . . . . . . . . . . . . . . . . . . . . . . . . . . . . . . . . . . . . . . . . . . . . .

2 cups (473 ml) chicken broth

2 cups (473 ml) heavy cream

2 tbsp (20 g) garlic, minced

½ cup (115 g) butter

½ cup (50 g) all-purpose flour

2 cups (360 g) Parmesan cheese, shredded

Place all of the ingredients in the slow cooker. Gently stir together and stir occasionally.

Cook on low for 4 to 6 hours.

# PEACH BUTTER

A delightful sweet and smooth spread you'll want to put on everything!
Fresh peaches are perfect in desserts like cobbler and pies, but there's so much more
you can do with them. This spread will leave your family asking for more!

**MAKES 20 SERVINGS**

20 peaches, ripe and sliced

2 cups (383 g) sugar

1 tbsp (7.5 g) cinnamon

½ tsp cloves

Place all of the ingredients in the slow cooker.

Cook on low for 6 to 8 hours.

# STRAWBERRY APPLESAUCE

A yummy twist to traditional applesauce that will be quite pleasing for all! Only four ingredients makes this a go-to recipe for fresh applesauce. Another bonus is that all the ingredients are healthy picks your body craves!

**MAKES 8 TO 10 SERVINGS**

6 cups (750 g) apples, chopped

1 cup (166 g) strawberries, sliced

4 tbsp (60 ml) honey

½ cup (118 ml) water

Place all of the ingredients in the slow cooker.

Cook on low for 8 to 10 hours or on high for 6 to 8 hours.

If you don't have apples, substitute with applesauce!

# DRINKS *for* A CROWD

I'll always remember my mom making slow cooker hot chocolate for our Christmas parties. It was a creamy, delicious chocolatey drink that we topped with whipped cream. No one could get enough of it! Ever since then, I've looked for easy slow cooker drinks to make at holidays or get-togethers. This is a great way to make a large amount easily!

# HOLIDAY CRANBERRY APPLE CIDER

The taste of sweet apples and crisp cranberries with a hint of cinnamon makes this a favorite holiday drink. Make your memories each year with the aromas of cinnamon, cranberry and apple. Your family will instantly have smiles on their faces!

**MAKES 12 TO 14 SERVINGS**

4 cups (1 L) apple juice

4 cups (1 L) cranberry juice

2 cups (473 ml) orange juice

½ cup (96 g) sugar

3 tsp (7.5 g) cinnamon

Pour all of the ingredients into the slow cooker. Gently stir together.

Cook on low for 3 to 4 hours.

Add cinnamon sticks or spike with cinnamon schnapps!

# PEANUT BUTTER HOT COCOA

This delicious drink is every peanut butter lover's dream come true, and your guests will wonder how you made it. Sometimes this drink is even better than dessert!

**MAKES 12 TO 14 SERVINGS**

. . . . . . . . . . . . . . . . . . . . . . . . . . . . . . . . . . . . . . . . . . . . . . . . . . .

6 cups (1.5 L) milk

½ cup (65 g) **cocoa powder**

1 cup (130 g) **powdered sugar**

½ cup (90 g) peanut butter

1 tsp vanilla

¼ cup (60 ml) **chocolate sauce**

Whipped cream, chocolate syrup, for serving

Pour all of the ingredients into the slow cooker. Gently stir together.

Cook on low for 3 to 4 hours or on high for 2 hours.

Top with whipped cream and chocolate syrup!

# TRIPLE HOT CHOCOLATE FOR A CROWD

This heavenly hot chocolate is the perfect go-to drink if you're expecting a lot of people. From kids to adults, all will love this homemade drink! Dip your favorite vanilla cookie in your drink for an additional snack!

**MAKES 18 TO 20 SERVINGS**

2 cups (473 ml) coffee creamer

1 (11.5-oz [326-g]) bag milk chocolate chips

1 (11.5-oz [326-g]) bag semisweet chocolate chips

¼ cup (27.8 g) cocoa powder

1 (14-oz [397-g]) can sweetened condensed milk

6 cups (1.5 L) milk

Place all of the ingredients in the slow cooker. Gently stir together.

Cook on low for 6 to 8 hours or on high for 3 to 4 hours.

Peppermint coffee creamer is amazing in this!

# VANILLA LATTE

Your favorite vanilla latte is easy to make with your regular coffee machine and a couple of extra ingredients. You'll be happy you get to sip these wonderful flavors!

**MAKES 12 TO 14 SERVINGS**

3 cups (710 ml) brewed coffee

2 cups (473 ml) milk

3 tbsp (45 ml) vanilla

¼ cup (60 ml) white chocolate sauce

Whipped cream, for serving

Pour all of the ingredients into the slow cooker. Gently stir together.

Cook on low for 4 hours.

Top with whipped cream!

ACKNOWLEDGMENTS

Eric—Thank you for always being there. Without you, none of this would be possible. You have always brought out the best in me. I love you, always.

Joey and Blake—Thank you for being the most wonderful boys. I couldn't ask for better kids to call my own. I love you guys!

Mom and Dad—Thank you for instilling a solid work ethic in me. Without you I wouldn't have a successful business and would have given up years ago.

Marcia and Kendall—Thank you for always treating and supporting me like your own daughter. I can't imagine any better in-laws.

Elisha and Rachel—This book wouldn't be here today without you. Thank you for all your help!

Will and Liz—Thank you for allowing me to share my recipes!

Ted—The photos in the book are beautiful! Thank you for making my recipes look so delicious!

ABOUT THE AUTHOR

Chrissy Taylor has been married to her high school sweetheart, Eric, for twenty years. Together they've had two active boys, Joey and Blake. After eighteen years of living away from their hometown, they recently moved back to rural Iowa to be closer to their family and friends.

Chrissy has been an online influencer with a successful lifestyle blog, The Taylor House, for the last five years. She's shared hundreds of recipes with her readers while working alongside national brands to incorporate their products into her recipes. Chrissy has also made an appearance on *Good Morning America* and has her recipes featured on *Woman's Day, Country Living* and *Cosmopolitan*.

You can follow along with her future recipes and work on her website, www.thetaylor-house.com!

INDEX